Praise for MOSQUITO RAIN

"With his clear, vivid narrative and deep humanity, Dan Szczesny invites us to join him and his wife, Meenakshi, as they ride in their small SUV along Alaskan highways and back roads, camping in the ceaseless light of summer wherever the journey takes them — a Walmart parking lot populated with fellow campers, the wilderness of Denali National Park, the interior of the Worthington Glacier, the Yukon River, the Arctic Circle, and astonishing settings in between. Amid a wilderness both achingly beautiful and treacherous, the spirit finds sustenance in the teeming salmon and the wind, in the mineral water of the melting glacier, and in the unforeseen."

~ William O'Daly, author of *The Road to Isla Negra*
and translator of Pablo Neruda's *World's End*

MOSQUITO RAIN

Alaskan Travel Essays by
Dan Szczesny

FOLDED WORD
Meredith

Copyright ©2016 by Dan Szczesny

All rights reserved. No part of this publication may be reproduced or distributed in any form or by any means, electronic or mechanical, without prior permission in writing from the publisher. Publisher hereby grants permission to reviewers to quote up to five hundred words in their reviews, and requests that hyperlinks to said reviews be e-mailed or physical copies mailed to the address below.

Requests for permission to make copies of any part of this work should be e-mailed to:
    editors@foldedword.com, subject line "permissions"

ISBN-13: 978-1-61019-226-2

Folded Word
79 Tracy Way
Meredith, NH 03253
United States of America
www.foldedword.com

Photographs by Meenakshi Gyawali
Map and glyphs by Megan Graustein
Design by JS Graustein
Titles set in Sitka
Text set in Garamond Premier Pro

*To Uma Moon —
someday, we'll return together*

Author's Note

I try to stay off the beaten path when I travel. More adventure. More authentic. Better food.

But what my wife, Meenakshi, and I learned very quickly was that Alaska itself *is* off the beaten path. All of it. It didn't take us long to realize that we could sleep just about anywhere — pull the car over next to the nearest river or mountain, crawl in back and you have an instant camping spot. And since it never got dark, we hardly wanted to sleep anyway.

So we drove as we liked, stopped when we wanted to, and discovered a whole different world of adventure from our native New Hampshire. When a local mentioned bears and cubs on the other side of Valdez Bay, we ran to the car and went there. When a fisherman told us about a secret salmon hot spot where fish swim right into the nets, we didn't hesitate. Walk into a glacier? Check. Smell the fire weed on the tundra? Got it. Blow a tire and a donut along the Denali Highway? Did that too.

We made this adventure up as we went; and in return, Alaska changed us. We came back filled with wonder and awe, and I wanted to bring a little bit of that wonder back with me.

This is our story of discovery as we searched Alaska, high and low, for the true meaning of its nickname: the Last Frontier. Given that Texas could easily fit inside Alaska, our search — as wide-ranging as it might have been — barely scratched the surface.

The route changes each time we travel, as does the land. But our plan always stays the same: Find adventure. Hope you enjoy what we found.

> ~ Dan Szczesny
> *Manchester, New Hampshire*
> *January 2016*

Meeting the Worthington Glacier

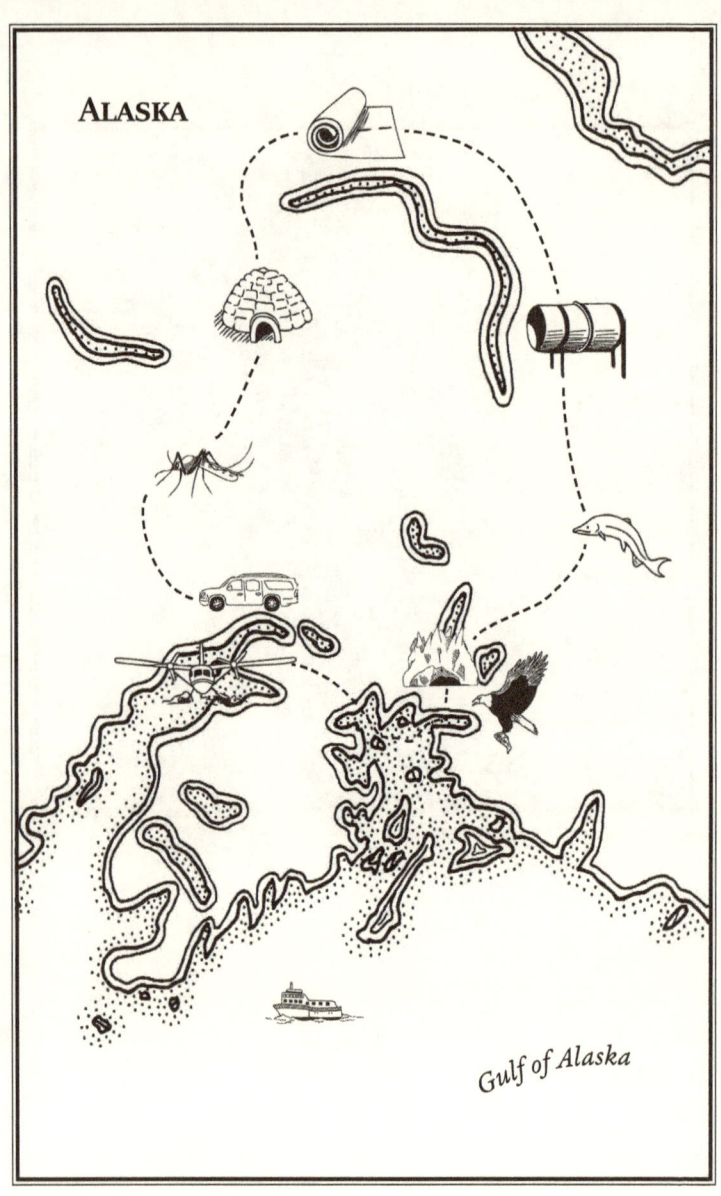

LEGEND & TABLE OF CONTENTS

	Concrete Camping *Wasilla*	1
	Mosquito Rain *Denali National Park*	7
	Searching for the Copper Salmon *Wrangell St. Elias National Park*	15
	Touching an Ice Age *North of Valdez*	23
	Putting Alaska Behind Us *Valdez & Valdez Bay*	29

(continued)

Notes from Alaska		35
	Tundra Road	36
	Rolling Out the Red Carpet	39
	Arctic Circle	
	In the Shadow of the Pipeline	40
	The Yukon Awaits	43
	South of the Arctic Circle	
	Thai Warmth	44
	Valdez	
	Ghosts of the Igloo	47
	North of Denali	
	Finding Peace	48
	Anchorage	
About the Author		51
Acknowledgements		52

MOSQUITO RAIN

CONCRETE CAMPING

*Of endless sun, picking the right parking space
and shaving at a Wal-Mart*

We're trying to get some sleep in a Super Wal-Mart parking lot in Wasilla.

Yes, that Wasilla; but unlike former Mayor Sarah Palin, we cannot see Russia from here. In fact, we can't see much of anything because we have jury-rigged curtains around the inside-back of our SUV. It's 1 AM and we're trying to keep the sun out.

We promised ourselves before arriving that this trip would be basic and raw. We didn't want to sleep in a hotel, we wanted to be closer to the earth, closer to the mountains and lakes. We wanted to find the Alaska of our imagination and we reasoned that we would not be able to find that at a Motel 6.

In all our travels, we have never experienced 22-hour sun days and our bodies are just not getting the proper signals that it's time to go to sleep. Alaska is so big, and the spaces between places so vast, that you can be tricked into being awake long past when you should be snoring. Normally on road trips, you'd drive till it gets dark. But what if it doesn't get dark?

We've found that Alaska is designed for just such situations. Roads and highways are marked with pull offs, parking areas, and shelters; most of them sit by rivers or next to soaring mountain passes. Even in the middle of nowhere, we have been able to stop and sleep or nap and enjoy some sort of wilderness view. And in most towns, big or small, there are laundromats designed with travelers in mind: Wash a load and take a shower while you are waiting for your clothes to dry.

Try pulling off the side of the road and taking a nap in New Hampshire and a state trooper will be knocking on your window in about five minutes. Yet Alaska is entirely comfortable with and understanding about makeshift camp sites. Especially at Wal-Mart.

It took me a while to warm to the idea of sleeping at a Wal-Mart. But here in the bigger cities (Wasilla is the seventh largest in Alaska), this makes the most sense. Yes, down in the lower 48 there are Wal-Marts and there are SUVs and campers that overnight in the parking lot. In fact, NASCAR race days in New Hampshire are one of our biggest Super Wal-Mart overnight days. But in Alaska, where the day never ends and the mystery of the

Concrete Camping

Last Frontier permeates every fiber of the state's identity, Wal-Mart camping is a rite of passage.

Their lots are huge and sections are clearly delineated for the big campers and smaller cars like ours. And since these Wal-Marts are open 24 hours, those 3 AM bathroom breaks are easy. Though I admit that walking through a bright parking lot so early in the morning and saying hello to other campers eating late night snacks on aluminum picnic tables just to use the bathroom in a nearly empty box store can be a bit surreal. But the employees all seem perfectly used to such activity. Inside the store, on benches behind the registers, other campers are sitting and reading, while their phones charge in outlets along the wall. Still others, in sweats and pajama tops, are waiting in line to buy snacks or soda.

The mood is casual and I feel silly. But I still use the chance to brush my teeth and give myself a quick shave. I have no idea how many more opportunities I'll have once we head north toward Denali.

Back at the SUV, we've shoved all our gear into the front seats; and with the back seats down, I can nearly perfectly fit head to toe stretched out in the back. Meena, of course, has plenty of room. We string some bungee cords around the hanger hooks and toss towels over them to block out the sun, which never quite sets.

There settles upon us a sort of gypsy freedom, different

from the freedom of a backpack or tent. This is a sort of communion with concrete, the ultimate getting away from and being in the middle of western civilization at the same time. We're here in a familiar space — what's more familiar to an American than a parking lot — surrounded by comfortable mile posts. The strip, fast food joints, four lanes — all the trappings of the most identifiable place in every city in every state.

And yet, maybe it's the sun that never seems to set. Maybe it's the hint of high, unnamed mountains on the horizon. Maybe it's this strange community of humans from all over the globe, sleeping in the backs of trucks and cars and teardrops and campers, each of them looking ahead to the unknown. With them, together, pavement or not, the lot is thick with an air of anticipation. There are adventures to be had, wonders to behold.

Tomorrow.

For tonight, I lay my head down on a folded-up jacket and look out the cracks behind the towels and watch the sun, now (and seemingly forever) a beacon on the horizon, while the white glow from the Wal-Mart sign helps me drift off to sleep.

Denali, Maker of Clouds

MOSQUITO RAIN

We search for a good stiff breeze in Denali National Park

In the morning, we are awoken by what sounds like raindrops hitting our tent. It's nice.

We're deep into Denali National Park, 85 miles deep, at Wonder Lake Campground. A camper bus took half a day to get us here. The ride was long, but magnificent.

Our goal was to camp in the shadow of Denali, the towering jut of ice and rock formally known as Mount McKinley and the highest mountain in North America. And here, at the farthest point of this campground — they call our spot the honeymoon suite — we wake expecting that white mountain to be shining like a small moon above our tent.

But Denali does not show itself. Nearby forest fires have turned the air hazy, and deep into this valley — surrounded by dozens of crisscrossing swamps, inlets, and ponds — the air is thick with moisture.

Mosquito Rain

Oh, and the raindrops? Mosquitoes. They swarm in thick black swirls above us, pelting the tent. We have never, not even during the most humid days of summer in the deepest wetlands of New Hampshire, experienced mosquitoes like this. Step out of the tent and they are on you instantly. Bug dope appears to have no effect. They swarm around our head nets, angry, desperate for blood.

Meena and I break down our tent as quickly as we can, but even the few moments my hands are exposed are enough for me to come away with a dozen welts. I look in horror at my wife's back as she bends over to stuff the tent. There are easily a hundred mosquitoes on her fleece.

We cut our Wonder Lake camping plans short and resolve to get on the next bus out of here. Our trip into Denali becomes a search for wind. That's all. Just a breeze, someplace where we can hike to enjoy the views without being devoured.

A ranger tells us of a bluff 20 miles away near the Eielson Visitor Center where the wind blows and the views sing. We passed through it on the way to the campground and are happy to go back.

There is only one road in and out of this enormous park. Most of it is dirt, much of it is rough, and it's the only way you can get in here on wheels. Not your own wheels, either. Only the first 15 miles are accessible with your own car. The rest of it requires a camp or resort bus.

Mosquito Rain

In a few hours, we're at the center — easily the most splendid visitor center we have ever seen, named for Carl Ben Eielson. Eielson was an early 20th-century aviator and bush pilot and the first guy to fly across the Arctic Ocean. He died in a spectacular and highly publicized attempt to rescue explorer Olaf Swenson in Siberia. Swenson's ship, the *Nanuk*, was trapped in ice and Eielson flew out to deliver furs and supplies. But he flew into a storm and a faulty altimeter is to blame for his flying straight into the ground with a wide-open throttle. In took about a year to recover his body from the ice.

Hoping to see some ice ourselves, we set our sights on the bluffs above the center. There's about two miles of trail to get up there, but we have an extra half day because of our escape from Wonder Lake; and even though Denali has not revealed itself, the valley around the center is clear and breathtaking.

We move up the trail slowly, our legs sluggish not from elevation but from inaction. This is our first real hike of the trip. There are signs everywhere warning of grizzlies, so our bear bells chime pleasantly as we begin the stiff climb to the top. The bluff is mostly open alpine, but there are a few blind turns around some switchbacks.

We've heard stories all week from hikers and locals alike of how bear bells no longer work, how the bears have come to identify tinkling bells not as something to stay away from, but rather as something that means food is coming. I ask a ranger about this later and he just shrugs and suggests that the next time we hike, we talk or sing as we go.

As we climb, the McKinley River Valley opens up under us. To the south, the Muldrow Glacier comes down off the mountain, its icy tongue sparkling like silver in the undercast. Directly below us, the river breaks into dozens of braids, fed by water coming from all different sources and spilling into the Tuklat River.

Mist rises up from the lower Alaska Range, and with every few feet of elevation we gain, the landscape seems to change, opening wider to reveal layers of mountains and glaciers spreading out in every direction. Many of these mountains are not even named, are simply foothills.

As we climb, the wind picks up speed. It never gets too cold, but we can feel the glacial breeze crawling up our bluff. When it hits us, it feels like it's coming from an air conditioner, which, when you think about it, is what Mt. Denali is to this place.

We are surrounded by wild flowers, many of which we have not seen before. After an hour or so, we breach the top of the bluff and are amazed to discover not a ridge, but a colorful alpine plateau spreading to the north toward the Kantishna and Wyoming hills.

I'm also surprised to discover a half dozen other hikers up here: Perhaps there are other routes up to this bluff?

Mosquito Rain

The wind is fierce and sustained. It blows so hard, Meena spreads her arms and leans down toward the ground. The wind holds her up. We stumble across the plateau like children learning to walk, and equally as giddy. Despite the fact that we are not alone, this is the Denali we've come to see. This is the place in our imagination.

There are beaten paths here and there. We pick one that appears to head up to a craggy outcropping, sort of a point atop the plateau. We pick our way against the wind over copper-colored rocks, and as we top out, the lower flanks of Denali reveal themselves across the valley, its serrated ice shelves shooting straight up into swirling, heavy clouds.

The wind howls in our ears and we hold on to each other, both for support and just out of sheer joy. The force of the gusts causes my eyes to water and burns my cheeks, but I could not be any happier here at 5,000 feet.

For a few glorious moments, Denali is ours.

Mosquito Rain

Fileting salmon on the banks of the Copper River

Searching for the Copper Salmon of O'Brian Creek

We find an Alaskan side road to a local, and secret, fishing hotspot

From a mysterious fisherman in rubber boots with deep lines in his forehead, we catch word of a secret cove where locals pull salmon from the water: a place called O'Brian Creek.

I'm struggling to flame my Jetboil when he wanders by, amused by my failing efforts. I'm starving, and sick of the Nepali trail mix and apples we've been eating all week. I badly want to warm up my bagged potato soup, but I'll eat it cold if I have to.

Meenakshi and I have been meandering through Alaska like gypsies this past week, rolling our SUV into parking lots or turn-offs and camping when the sun gets low enough to let the sky pass for night. But it's hard to sleep when there's no night, and it's harder still when around every turn is an unexpected adventure. We blew a tire on the Denali Highway and had to sleep in the back one night — at 3,000 feet with a storm moving through and giant craggy mountains around us. Then we blew the donut on the way back out and made friends with a native tow-truck driver who patched us up enough so we could limp into Fairbanks. Now we're in the sparsely populated southeast part of the state, close to the Yukon and near the entrance to Wrangell-St. Elias National Park — trying to eat something, trying to figure out where to go next — when we hear of this place not too far away, where the prized Copper River salmon flows in prolific runs.

He has his own bucket of salmon, our fisherman, and we stand along the side of the road with him for a while and watch a large Filipino family pull fish after fish out of the Copper River using long dip-nets. The men wade out there in a huge half-circle, sometimes up to their chests in the strong current, and pull the wide nets along. By the time they reach the other side of the circuit, they have two, sometimes three salmon, pulling and straining to get out. Those fish, mindless in their desire to spawn, swim right into the nets. Once they're ashore, the women bash them with a wrench and the whole fish goes in a bucket. This goes on for hours, collecting enough to feed that whole family the rest of the year.

"You should see this shore during the day," our fisherman muses. "It's like little Manila out there." Indeed,

Searching for the Copper Salmon

Alaska has one of the largest Filipino populations in the States. And this family, at least, has had a good day.

With midnight approaching, we leave our fisherman and scurry back through Chitina, a town of about 150 with its back broken, looking for renewal. Around 1900, Chitina sprung up from the ashes of an indigenous Athabaskan village after copper ore was discovered in the valley. Now, Chitina sits at a crossroads: The opportunity to be the main village of a newly founded national park could put the place on the map.

We find the dirt side road and rumble along toward O'Brian Creek, mapless and uncertain what we're looking for. We drive past a couple RV pull-offs crowded with beaten-down campers and muddy children playing next to rusty grills. The road gets bad, and thin, and we swing around the side of a hill rising straight up from the river below. There's another pull-off at the top, carved right out of the dirt. We get out to have a look around, and then we see O'Brian Creek below us.

The creek has carved a path between two craggy hills, pouring down from up-valley and roaring into the Copper River. In the space between the hills is a rocky mud flat. And along that mud flat is a busy ant-hive of a fishing operation. Dozens of fishermen have created a surreal community, hanging on to the sides of those hills. ATVs tear hell across the rocks. There are a couple port-a-johns and, incredibly, a shed-sized shack that sells espresso. A few people are relaxing in front of fires, and tents are sprinkled along the cove here and there.

We're unwilling to risk another blowout, so we park up on the rise and hoof it down to the flats, where we wander around in a daze. Across the swiftly moving river, the foothills of the national park seem to rise straight up out of the reddish water.

In New Hampshire, where we live, this place would be designated a scenic area and protected. It would be a White Mountain highlight and appear on tourist maps and literature. Here, it is a place of sustenance living: an achingly beautiful, yet practical, dent in the river, pushed back from the current enough to allow fishermen to cast or dip their nets.

All along the shore, women and men in various states of dress, from full waders and wetsuits to jean shorts and sneakers, try their luck. And this year, the spawn is not disappointing. The fish are practically jumping into the nets. One man is using his big red cooler as a cutting table, turning the fish into fresh filets almost as soon as they are pulled from the water.

Elsewhere, all along the creek as it pours down from the mountain, cutting tables are set up along the banks. The fish are taken directly to the tables, where locals gut them and slice them into pink strips. Unlike the immigrants up river, these men toss the fish remains into the creek to either flow out into the Copper or get washed ashore nearby. At the junction of the two waters, thousands of seagulls squawk and fitter about, feasting on the salmon graveyard.

The sun is now behind the mountain horizon and provides a calm, casual vibe to this odd and wonderful place. It's nearly 1 AM. Echoes of ATVs in the surrounding hills bounce down into the cove, and somebody deep in the forest is laughing too loud.

We head back up to our car and sit on a rock overlooking the river to watch the cove from above. Before too long, another couple of cars join us, and the fires below begin to die down. It appears the day is at an end. The smell of blood and fire and mountain air drifts up to our perch giving me chills and peace. And for once, sleep comes easy this night, here among the salmon ghosts.

Mosquito Rain

Inside the Worthington Glacier

Touching an Ice Age
on the Road to Valdez

We continue our Alaskan search for discovery
by hiking into a glacier

Near the bottom of the Worthington Glacier, where the runoff evens out into a small pond before continuing into the valley, there sits a single cairn.

I pause for a moment here. My wife has already begun the hike across the braided inlets toward the foot of the glacier itself. But I can't help wondering: *Why was this cairn built?*

It makes a fine picture, aligned as it is with the towering glacier. Perhaps it marks some past geological border from which the glacier has retreated.

Or, more romantically, perhaps this single cairn is not a way-mark at all. Maybe the pile of rocks is a stop sign, meant to encourage wanderers like us to pause and fully appreciate our place at the foot of an ice age.

Mosquito Rain

We are not far off the beaten path this time. The Worthington Glacier is one of the most popular tourist spots along the Richardson Highway, deep in the Copper River Basin. We are en route to Valdez, and once we came down off Thompson Pass and began the long turn to the south, the Worthington was impossible to miss from the highway.

Still, as crowded as the information stand and view pad of this state recreation site are, few appear to have any stomach today for the extra, unmarked mile hike of moraine and glacial runoff that is required to get close, or even touch the thing. Perhaps the raw, icy rain up here in the Chugash Mountains is keeping the tourists at bay.

That's fine with me. The chilling and blustery rain lends the glacier a faraway, dangerous feel. The bad weather makes Worthington feel like it's not one of the most highway-accessible glaciers in the world. As we begin the final scramble up the glacier wall, it feels like the rest of the world could be a thousand miles away, or nowhere at all.

Worthington's immediate history is sketchy. The glacier is named after a surveyor who was part of an 1899 team sent up from Valdez to find a route over the passes into the territory's interior. He has no first name, or perhaps Worthington is his first name, but part of his legend is that he survived being swept away in a glacial stream — maybe this very stream.

Touching an Ice Age

The trail narrows as we approach the glacier head wall. On one side is Mount Billy Mitchell, a nearly 7,000-foot hill. The ice pours down off this mountain in a 5,000-acre-plus blast of Ice Age snow crystals. The glacier is melting, of course, and the roar of water pouring over the top and tearing down Billy Mitchell's walls is deafening. We inch our way over loose scree and crumbling rock, the glacier melt roaring down a slot flume to our right. One slip here and we'd be washed right back into that glacier pond with the cairn.

To our left, the glacier wall grows higher and higher. Soon we are in a canyon: the glacier on one side, the mountain on the other. Icy mist sprays from a hundred different spots, like the glacier is leaking.

We find a thin entrance, a sideways crevasse where we can walk straight into the glacier's mouth. The hole is not wide enough for two people, so we have to take turns. Here, inside the glacier at eye level, the ice is bright blue. I take off my gloves and run my hand along the glacier's wall, smooth as marble.

I'm surprised by how quiet it is in here. Looking up, high above me the blue ice thins into an arched ceiling of ice. I sidestep as deeply into the slot as I can, but soon find the walls closing around me. I stand here, tiny. I am barely a blink of an eye to this monster, this grinding creature that has existed for thousands of years.

Mosquito Rain

To be fair, even though the glacier itself has existed since the last Ice Age, this particular piece of glacial ice is only a hundred years old or so. But that little myth-busting factoid in the back of my brain doesn't defuse the experience any. This thing is too big to let geology get in the way of thoughts on greater purpose and our relatively miniscule place in this world.

We move out of the glacier, and I want to try one last thing. I cup my hands under an icy ledge where water runs off freely and bring the liquid to my lips. And just like that, the glacier and I become one. It tastes a bit gravelly and I hope there are no glacier worms in this bit of water, but it is almost sweet. The water drips off my beard and a bit gets under my jacket and runs down my neck. I look out and down the alley — the same view that this glacier has had for a long, long time — and feel comfortable about my place in the world...

...small though it may be.

The Port of Valdez

PUTTING ALASKA BEHIND US
IN PRINCE EDWARD SOUND

*We reach the end of the pipeline in Valdez,
and find much more than oil*

I stare up at the giant metal salmon sculpture. From this perspective, near the visitor center, the fish looms over the massive mountains that surround Valdez.

Yes, that Valdez. The Valdez permanently seared into our memories by pictures of oil-slicked seals and rescue crews desperately trying to save thousands of creatures after the Exxon Valdez ran aground on a reef in Prince William Sound and spilled millions of gallons of crude into the bay.

As an aside, here are two facts about that incident you might not know: (1) The captain of the vessel, the much-maligned Joseph Hazelwood, was indeed drunk when the ship ran aground, but he was not at the controls. He was sleeping off his bender in his bunk. No matter, Exxon blamed him anyway. (2) The Exxon Valdez was put back into service under a different name, served under several different flags and currently awaits dismantling at the tide-flooded Alang Ship Recycling Yard in India. The last name the vessel had? *The Oriental Nicety*. Weird, right?

Anyway, I'm not thinking at all about oil spills as we wander around Valdez. I'm thinking about what a strange and wonderful place this is. We have nearly a full 24 hours to wander the town's streets, past the fishing vessels, across the pedestrian bridge that leads to the town's main strip, and along the docks where moms toss lines with little kids in tow and older couples hold hands and look up at the mountain ridges.

There are hole-in-the-wall crab shacks, Chinese takeout dens and espresso trucks catering to everyone from Westerners whose boots smell like the fishing derby they just finished to young eastern twentysomethings in Madison Ave styles and big round sunglasses.

We meet a bearded scraggly local with a portfolio of his photography. He's just wandering the streets. His stuff is good, actually.

"These visitor center phonies, they ain't from here," he says, spitting his chewed up cigar into a gutter. "I been here all my life. Right now, up at the end of the oil line, there's a grizzly and some cubs. I heard tourists are heading up there."

We don't even question the info, but run to our car and

bee-line out of town. Valdez sits at the north side of Port Valdez, the bay. On the other side, the Alaskan pipeline terminates. In between the two are miles of bay shore, RV parks, glacier bays and wetlands.

The day is cold. Low mist and humid clouds slash across the surrounding mountains, giving the bay a surreal, quiet feel. The tide is out, and rolls of mud flats carve thousands of little islands and perches near the water. As it turns out, there are no bears, but we stop anyway, in awe of what *is* out there.

A dozen bald eagles swoop and play out on the water. As they bring little fish out of the water to their nests deep within the pines, they soar directly over our heads. In New Hampshire, a single eagle sighting is likely to be the lead story on the evening news. Here, there are a dozen. Several bald eaglets hop around the mud — ugly, fuzzy little things squawking for food. They don't have the white head plumes of their parents yet.

As if this display is not enough, a raft of sea otters suddenly appears, their big round eyes popping above the water long enough, seemingly, to stare down the incredulous humans on the shore before continuing their forage.

I have never seen anything like this.

It would be easy to sit here all day and stare at the eagles, but we need to book passage aboard a ferry that will

Mosquito Rain

take us through Prince Edward Sound and back toward Anchorage.

On the way back to Valdez, we pass the site of old Valdez. The entire town was moved in 1964 after what's come to be known as the Good Friday Earthquake. An incredible 9.2 earthquake rocked southern Alaska that day. It didn't immediately or directly harm Valdez, but it liquefied the underlying glacier silt, creating an underwater landslide that eventually destroyed the port and a large portion of the town. So they moved the town six miles down bay.

We end our day camping out in the back of our car near the ferry terminal, accompanied by the sound of gulls and the low glare of the terminal port in the night.

The next morning, ours is one of the first cars loaded up onto the M/V *Aurora*. The ferry will take us on our final leg of the trip, through the sound and back to Whittier, a little port town just south of Anchorage. The voyage promises glacier views and soaring scenery. But in the gloom and undercast of the day, we get something much more. A half hour into the voyage, we put on our rain gear to protect against the icy sleet that sprinkles down from the mountains. The viewing deck is empty now, everyone else apparently content to see the misty mountains from behind glass. We walk aft to the end of the vessel, careful not to slip on the slick deck, and watch Valdez recede.

Putting Alaska Behind Us

We move through Prince William Sound like our presence here is a secret. Every little while, the sharp, icy flank of a nearby ridge pierces the mist and we fall quiet, not daring to alert the mountains to our intrusion. The waters around our little boat are filled with small glacier islands, bobbing by like deep blue mines.

From this distance, with the icy-white mountains and the rocky inlets jabbing into the water, Valdez looks perilous. As our ferry leaves, I can't help thinking that we, humans, are barely hanging on here — that with one careless shrug we'd be cast into the bay and the wilderness would not even notice.

Mosquito Rain

Notes from Alaska

Some final musings about the Last Frontier

Tundra Road

Along the Dalton Highway, there is a pull-off with a sign marking our entry into the Arctic Circle. It took us all morning to get here on a tour bus driven by a chipper, chatty local who informed us only upon our return that it was her first solo drive along the famed Ice Road. Yes, the *Ice Road Truckers* ice road. The road is dirt and hilly; but really, it doesn't seem nearly as awful as it's made out to be on that show. But then again, I just sat there in a plush seat, sipping soda.

Touching the Arctic

Rolling Out the Red Carpet

At the Arctic Circle sign, we step off the bus and our tour guide rolls out a red carpet with a dotted line down the middle. We all walk down that carpet, over the dotted line and into the Arctic Circle. Everybody poses in a variety of ways. It's cute, but somehow I want this experience to be more, I don't know, epic. The tundra up here is beautiful, but it doesn't feel like something we earned. I'm used to there being pain involved in accomplishment.

In the Shadow of the Pipeline

The Ice Road was built as a feeder road for the Trans-Alaskan Pipeline System, finished in 1974. But up here, just call it the pipeline. The pipeline casts its shadow over Alaska. It is ingrained in the consciousness and in the landscape of this magnificent place as deeply as though it were a mountain range. It is a stop for tourists, it provides access for hunters and hikers, it has created towns and roads where they otherwise would not exist. Alaskans appear proud and embarrassed at once over this 800-mile modern masterpiece. We stop along the Ice Road and everyone on the bus gets off and walks 50 yards to where the pipeline shoots by overhead and we take pictures. Then we all just mill about, waving away mosquitoes. After all, it's only a pipeline.

Under the Pipeline

The Yukon Awaits

Meena and I stroll along the Yukon River, about an hour south of the Arctic Circle. Along with the pipeline, an enormous bridge crosses at this junction — this truck stop where bikers and tourists and truckers mingle in the Yukon River Camp. They sell lunch here, egg sandwiches and chips and warm Pepsi. They also sell T-shirts and hats and patches and key chains, and rightfully so. This is my favorite place along the Dalton Highway — remote, wild, a melting pot at the end of the Earth. A woman sells bone jewelry from a corrugated shack just outside the camp. She lives up river and boats down here every day to meet Dalton Highway travelers. In the parking lot are dozens of pickups and SUVs, hunters, fishermen, explorers, all of them someplace remote now. Like us, except we have the tour bus.

Thai Warmth

Tucked in a corner parking lot at the edge of Valdez is Gloy's Thai Food trailer. A cardboard sign announces Veggie and Tofu Dishes and Curry. We turn our backs on the fish fries and crab bakes and bars. It's cold. A raw mist hangs over town and we need something to warm our bellies. It seems amazing that Gloy's Thai Food would be here, in this place, at the edge of glaciers. There are no seats and it's too cold to eat outside anyway. So we sit in our car and watch the lights of Valdez shimmer in the rain and eat our drunken noodles, which are indeed fresh and spicy. Next time, I think, the next time I'm here I'm going to find Gloy and thank her for giving this moment to me.

Snapshots of Valdez

Ghosts of the Igloo

Not far from Denali National Park, on an otherwise pristine stretch of road, we come across Igloo City. Or rather, the crumbling, beautiful remains of what was once imagined to be Igloo City. In the 1970s, Igloo City was meant to be a hotel, recreation center, gas station and rest stop. It was mostly built before regulators swooped in and shut it down over code violations. After that, Igloo City was abandoned, and the Alaskan wilderness has slowly been taking it back ever since. I walk a full circuit around the ghostly white shell, designed apparently as a tribute to the Inuit culture. In the back, away from the road, someone has spray painted "I luv you this big!" across the dilapidated structure. We're not used to ruins of this sort out here. It seems unlikely the igloo will be able to stand very many more Alaskan winters.

Finding Peace

The day before we are to leave Alaska, through a series of odd circumstances, we find ourselves south of Anchorage sitting by a remote lake, eating noodles. A brisk wind blows over the lake, which is surrounded by mountains. I don't know the name of the lake or the mountains. We sit with our backs propped up against a piece of driftwood, slurping spicy Ramen. There's not much left to say. We're tired, our bones ache, and our clothes are dirty. As it should be. Then, one last amazing thing. A bright red bush plane suddenly swoops out of the clouds and lands on the water right in front of us. The pilot coasts along the water for a bit, eases up on the throttle, and the plane gently pushes up against the shore 20 feet away from us. The pilot jumps out, walks up on shore and heads to the port-a-potty in the parking lot. A few minutes later, he's back in the plane after nodding our way with a smile; and off he goes. We watch in wonder as the plane lifts off, heads back around a mountain and is gone, the buzz of the engine drifting away until all we hear again is the splash of wind-pulled water against the shore.

Alone with an Igloo

About the Author

DAN SZCZESNY is a long-time journalist, travel writer, editor, and author living in New Hampshire. He began his career in Buffalo, New York. Since then, he has written for a wide variety of regional and national publications, including the *Main Line Times, Philadelphia Weekly, Christian Science Monitor, Princeton Packet, Pennsylvania Magazine, all4woman.com, Yahoo! Parenting* and *Huffington Post*. He writes a monthly column for the Folded Word blog and an occasional column for *Good Men Project* called "Modern Dad" about getting kids into nature and the challenges of being an older dad.

In 2000, he moved to New Hampshire to cover the Presidential Primary Election. In 2001, Dan became Associate Publisher of *The Hippo*, now the state's largest Arts and Entertainment journal. He's a member of the Appalachian Mountain Club's 4,000-footer club and has written extensively about the outdoors and hiking, including two travel memoirs and one collection of short fiction. He has camped in the Grand Canyon, hiked England's Coast to Coast Trail, trekked to Everest Base Camp in Nepal and traveled in Northern India with his ten-month-old daughter. For more information on Dan and his writing, visit: **www.danszczesny.com**

Acknowledgments

The author would like to thank the fishermen, hikers, artists, tour guides, bus drivers, sled runners, food truck operators, tow truck drivers and bush pilots who made these little musings possible.

Thanks to JS Graustein at Folded Word Press who believed in the book. Also, to my editor, Lisa Parsons who, as usual, made it better.

To my light, Uma. And to Meenakshi, my navigator through travels and life.

The publisher would like to thank Rose Auslander, Casey Tingle, Barbara Flaherty, Miran Reynolds, Maryka Gillis, Kristine Slentz, and Megan Graustein for their assistance at the press during this book's production.

Previous Titles by Dan Szczesny

The Adventures of Buffalo and Tough Cookie
Bondcliff Books, 2013

*The Nepal Chronicles: Marriage, Mountains and
Momos in the Highest Place on Earth*
Hobblebush Books, 2014

Sing, and Other Short Stories
Hobblebush Books, 2015

Like this chapbook?
SUBSCRIBE TO THE SERIES.

Receive a fun, quick read semi-monthly in your mailbox! Subscriptions to the 2016 Chapbook Series will be available through 30 November 2016:

    Full year (9 titles): $50*
    SPRING Poetry (3 titles): $20
    SUMMER Prose (3 titles): $23
    AUTUMN Nature (3 titles): $23

To order, please visit our chapbook blog at:

FOLDEDCHAPS.WORDPRESS.COM

The subscription offer for the current year is on top. Offer extends to back issues of the current chapbook year.

**Full year subscriptions are a $100 value. Free shipping in the USA.*

Titles included in the
2016 CHAPBOOK SERIES:

SPRING Poetry

Cosmophagy by David Oestreich
Points of Reference by Matthew James Babcock
Little Town gods by L. Ward Abel

SUMMER Prose

Mosquito Rain by Dan Szczesny
The Book of Wishful Thinking by Darla K. Crist
Orange Balloon by Samantha Priestley, illustrated by
    Megan Graustein

AUTUMN Nature

Watershed by Jean French
A Year Unfolding by Debbie Strange
WaterWays by JS Graustein *&* William O'Daly

MORE FROM THE FOLDED FAMILY

Worlds Apart
by Smitha Murthy *&* Dorothee Lang

Freight
by Mel Bosworth

Catherine Sophia's Elbow
by Darla K. Crist

Sophronia L.
by Tim Bridwell

Ephemeral
by Miguel Lupián
translated by Joseph Hutchison

For a complete list of our titles plus multi-media presentations from this book, visit the Folded Word website: WWW.FOLDEDWORD.COM

To report typographical errors or a defective copy of this book, email: EDITORS@FOLDEDWORD.COM

Want more information about our books, chapbooks, and zine? Want to connect with contributors from this book? No problem. Simply join us at a social media outlet near you:

 weblog: FOLDED.WORDPRESS.COM
 Facebook: WWW.FACEBOOK.COM/FOLDEDWORD
 Twitter: TWITTER.COM/FOLDEDWORD
 Goodreads: FOLDED WORD FAN CLUB

We love to hear from our readers. Just send your thoughts via email to editors@foldedword.com with the subject line "Mosquito Rain Feedback."

Cheers!

CPSIA information can be obtained
at www.ICGtesting.com
Printed in the USA
LVHW050930200120
644155LV00008B/1348